:oln Elementary School
620 Carolina St.
Vallejo, Ca. 94590

Lincoln Elementary School
620 Carolina St.
Vallejo, Ca. 94590

What Is Climate?

by Ellen Lawrence

Consultants:

Suzy Gazlay, MA
Recipient, Presidential Award for Excellence in Science Teaching

Kimberly Brenneman, PhD
National Institute for Early Education Research, Rutgers University
New Brunswick, New Jersey

BEARPORT
PUBLISHING

New York, New York

Credits

Cover, © AnetaPics/Shutterstock and © Eric Isselée/Shutterstock; 3, © Zeljko Radojko/Shutterstock; 4–5, © Ariadne Van Zandbergen/FLPA; 6, © Evgeny Tomeev/Shutterstock; 7T, © picturepartners/Shutterstock; 7, © MaszaS/Shutterstock; 8, © Sam Chadwick/Shutterstock; 9, © Wendy Dennis/FLPA; 10, © Christian Ziegler/Minden Pictures/FLPA; 11, © Wild Arctic Pictures/Shutterstock; 12T, © Pete Oxford/Minden Pictures/FLPA; 12B, © Michael & Patricia Fogden/Minden Pictures/FLPA; 13, © Dr. Morley Read/Shutterstock; 14, © Arto Hakola/Shutterstock; 15, © Larry Minden/Minden Pictures/FLPA; 16, © Yva Momatiuk & John Eastcott/Minden Pictures/FLPA; 17T, © Cosmographics; 17, © Michio Hoshino/Minden Pictures/FLPA; 18T, © Gail Johnson/Shutterstock; 18B, © Lusoimages/Shutterstock; 19, © Vladitto/Shutterstock; 19BR, © leonid_tit/Shutterstock; 20, © Jan Martin Will/Shutterstock; 21C, © Cosmographics; 21L, © Nataliya Hora/Shutterstock; 21T, © Patrick Poendl/Shutterstock; 21R, © EPA/Corbis; 21B, © Volodymyr Goinyk/Shutterstock; 22BL, © Sergey Smolin/Shutterstock; 22BC, © Eric Isselée/Shutterstock; 22BR, © Matt Jeppson/Shutterstock; 23TL, © Nataliya Hora/Shutterstock; 23TC, © Alexander Shadrin/Shutterstock; 23TR, © Stéphane Bidouze/Shutterstock; 23BL, © Gail Johnson/Shutterstock; 23BC, © Wild Arctic Pictures/Shutterstock; 23BR, © leonid_tit/Shutterstock.

Publisher: Kenn Goin
Senior Editor: Lisa Wiseman
Creative Director: Spencer Brinker
Design: Emma Randall
Editor: Mark J. Sachner
Photo Researcher: Ruby Tuesday Books Ltd.

Library of Congress Cataloging-in-Publication Data

Lawrence, Ellen, 1967-
  What is climate? / by Ellen Lawrence.
     p. cm. — (Weather wise)
  Includes bibliographical references and index.
  ISBN 978-1-61772-401-5 (library binding) — ISBN 1-61772-401-7 (library binding)
  1. Climatology—Juvenile literature. I. Title.
  QC981.3.L3955 2012
  551.6—dc23
                          2011049583

For more information, write to Bearport Publishing Company, Inc., 45 West 21st Street, Suite 3B, New York, New York 10010. Printed in the United States of America in North Mankato, Minnesota.

10 9 8 7 6 5 4 3 2 1

Contents

Welcome to Death Valley! 4

Weather and Climate 6

Figuring Out Climate.............. 8

Cold, Hot, Wet, or Dry?........... 10

A Tropical Climate.................12

A Hot Desert Climate 14

A Super-Cold Climate..............16

Not Too Hot, Not Too Cold!.......18

Climate Record Breakers......... 20

Science Lab.................... 22

Science Words 23

Index 24

Read More................... 24

Learn More Online.................. 24

About the Author 24

Welcome to Death Valley!

It is summer in Death Valley, California.

There has been no rain for months and it is very hot.

This weather is not unusual, however.

Death Valley is part of a **desert**.

Its climate has been hot and dry for thousands of years.

Death Valley

Some parts of Death Valley get only about two inches (5 cm) of rain in a whole year!

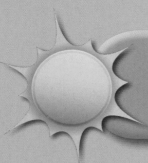

Weather and Climate

So is **weather** the same thing as climate?

No, weather is what happens in one place on a single day, or over a few days or weeks.

When it rains or snows, people say, "The weather is wet."

When it is very warm outside, people say, "The weather is hot."

Climate, on the other hand, is the type of weather a place has over 30 or more years.

For example, people say, "Death Valley has a desert climate."

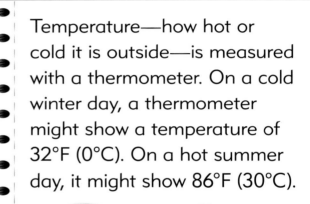

Temperature—how hot or cold it is outside—is measured with a thermometer. On a cold winter day, a thermometer might show a temperature of 32°F (0°C). On a hot summer day, it might show 86°F (30°C).

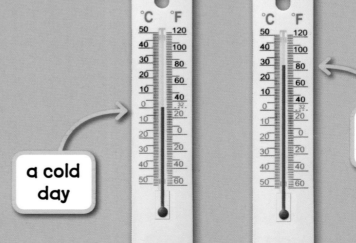

a cold day

a hot day

cold, snowy weather

hot, sunny weather

7

Figuring Out Climate

To figure out what type of climate a place has, scientists look at many years of weather records.

The records include daily temperatures and how much **precipitation** fell, if any.

Over 30 years, scientists may find that one area usually has hot summers and snowy winters.

Another area might be hot all year with very little rain.

New York has cold, snowy winters.

Describe your area's usual weather during each season. For example, you might say, "Summer is hot and dry." Then continue by describing the weather in the other seasons.

Scientists who study climate are called climatologists.

meerkats in the hot, dry climate of the Kalahari Desert in Africa

Cold, Hot, Wet, or Dry?

There are many different types of climate.

Some areas have a cold climate, while others have a hot climate.

Some places get lots of rain, while others get almost none.

Climate is what makes some places deserts and others **rain forests**.

In a hot place with so little rain that it's hard for plants to grow, a desert develops.

In a hot, very wet climate that is just right for plants, a rain forest grows.

rain forest

Wild animals have bodies that are right for the climate in which they live. Animals that live in cold climates, such as polar bears, have very thick fur to keep them warm.

polar bear

A Tropical Climate

A hot, wet climate is called a tropical climate.

In these places, the temperature may stay around 80°F (27°C) for most of the year.

About 75 to 100 inches (191 to 254 cm) of rain may fall every year, too!

The Amazon rain forest in South America has a tropical climate.

About 40,000 different types of trees and other plants grow there!

Rain forests are good places for animals to live because they offer shelter and plenty to eat. Over two million different types of insects live in the Amazon rain forest!

This Amazon rain forest insect is called a spiny katydid.

a macaw eating palm tree fruit

the trunk of a giant Amazon rain forest tree

13

A Hot Desert Climate

In a hot desert climate, the temperature may reach 120°F (49°C)—or hotter!

It is so dry that it might not rain for months.

As a result, plants and animals have to find ways to make water last longer.

Barrel cactuses can soak up enough water from a good rain to stay alive for several years!

Many animals, such as the desert tortoise, live underground to avoid the daytime sun.

They leave their homes to find food at night, when it's cooler.

a barrel cactus

A desert is a place that's very dry because it gets less than ten inches (25 cm) of rain or snow in a year. Some deserts are hot and dry, while others are cold and dry.

In what ways is a desert climate like the climate where you live? In what ways is it different?

entrance to underground home

desert tortoise

A Super-Cold Climate

Near the North Pole, the cold, dry desert-like climate has created a bare land called the **tundra**.

Hardly any rain and only a few inches of snow fall each year.

Winter temperatures may be as low as –94°F (–70°C).

The rocky ground stays frozen for most of the year, thawing a little each summer.

No trees can grow in this climate.

Only small low-growing plants can survive the cold and lack of water.

Caribou, a type of deer, live in large herds on the tundra. When snow covers the ground, they use their hooves to dig for plants to eat.

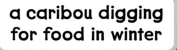

a caribou digging for food in winter

A desert can be hot and dry. The tundra is cold and dry. Which would you rather visit? Why?

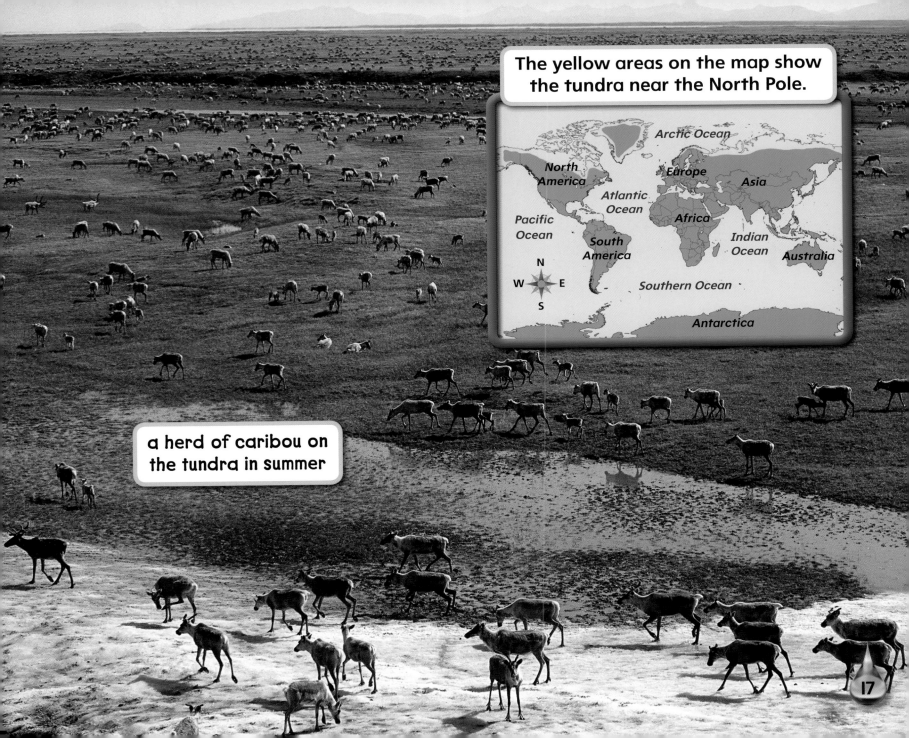

The yellow areas on the map show the tundra near the North Pole.

Arctic Ocean

North America

Europe

Asia

Atlantic Ocean

Pacific Ocean

Africa

South America

Indian Ocean

Australia

Southern Ocean

Antarctica

N W E S

a herd of caribou on the tundra in summer

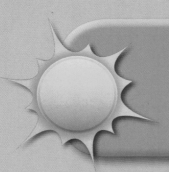

Places with a **temperate** climate do not have super-hot or super-cold temperatures.

As the seasons change, the weather changes.

It's warm in spring and hot in summer.

Fall is usually cooler than summer, and winter is cold.

Most people in North America live in areas with a temperate climate.

What season is it now where you live? Describe the weather.

spring in a temperate climate

summer in a temperate climate

fall in a temperate climate

winter in a
temperate climate

In an area with a temperate climate, it usually rains on and off all year. In winter, it might snow.

Climate Record Breakers

Some places have a climate that's extreme.

Check out these record-breaking climate events.

The map shows where these extreme events took place.

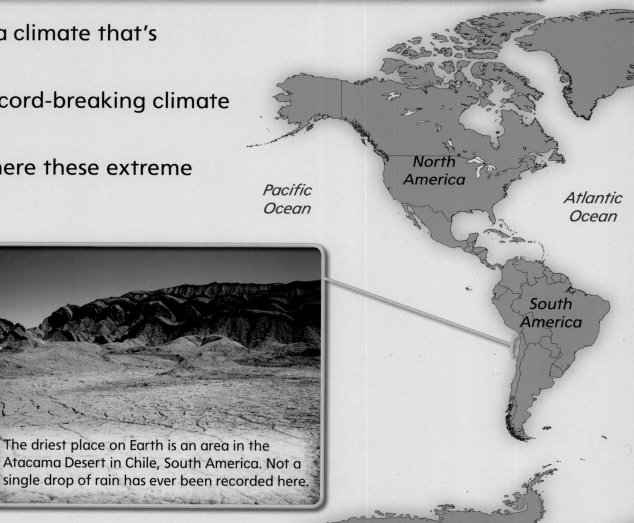

Pacific Ocean

North America

Atlantic Ocean

South America

The driest place on Earth is an area in the Atacama Desert in Chile, South America. Not a single drop of rain has ever been recorded here.

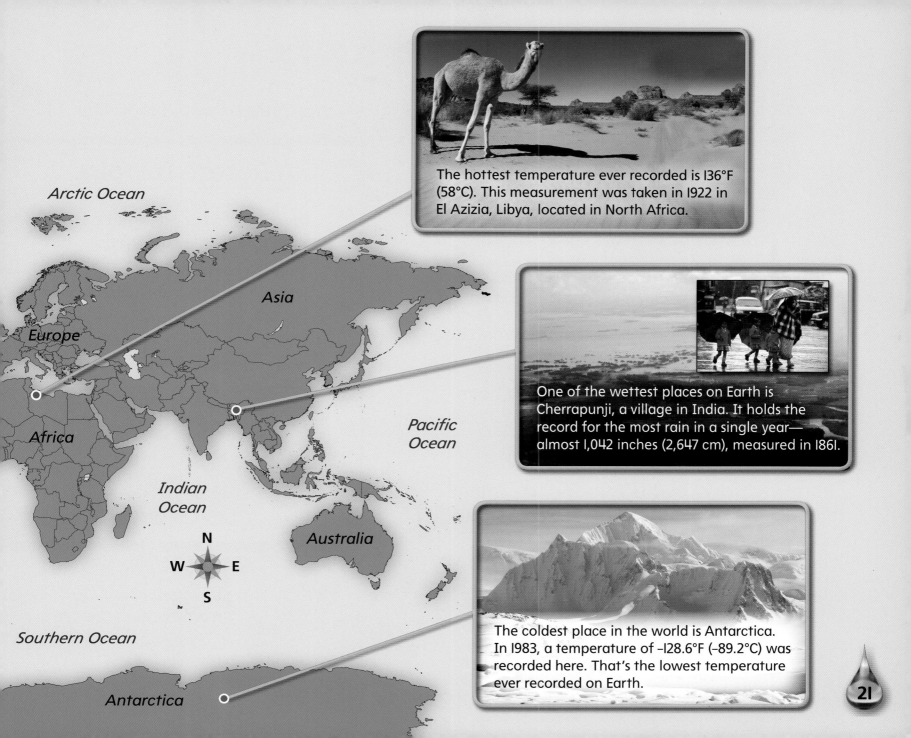

Arctic Ocean

Europe

Africa

Asia

Indian
Ocean

Australia

Pacific
Ocean

N
W · E
S

Southern Ocean

Antarctica

The hottest temperature ever recorded is 136°F (58°C). This measurement was taken in 1922 in El Azizia, Libya, located in North Africa.

One of the wettest places on Earth is Cherrapunji, a village in India. It holds the record for the most rain in a single year—almost 1,042 inches (2,647 cm), measured in 1861.

The coldest place in the world is Antarctica. In 1983, a temperature of –128.6°F (–89.2°C) was recorded here. That's the lowest temperature ever recorded on Earth.

Science Lab

Animals live and find their food in ways that are right for the climate in which they live.

Their bodies also develop in ways that help them live in that climate.

Be an Animal Scientist

Choose an animal that lives in a very cold climate, a hot desert, or a tropical rain forest.

Use the Internet and books to research the animal and its climate.

Then write a report about what you have learned.

Include pictures!

Share your report with your friends, family members, or teacher.

Your report could look like this:

A Desert Tortoise

Desert tortoises live in hot deserts where very little rain falls.

They dig underground homes where they can get shelter from the sun.

A desert tortoise can live for years without drinking water!

polar bear

rain forest tree frog

Science Words

desert (DEZ-urt) dry land with few plants and little rainfall; deserts are often covered with sand

precipitation (*pri*-sip-ih-TAY-shuhn) the different forms that water takes when it falls from a cloud; rain and snow are types of precipitation

rain forests (RAYN FOR-ists) warm places where many trees grow and lots of rain falls

temperate (TEM-pur-it) a climate with different seasons and few weather extremes compared to hot or cold climates

tundra (TUHN-druh) cold, treeless land where the ground is frozen just below the surface

weather (WETH-ur) how hot or cold it is outside, and other conditions such as rain, wind, and snow

Index

climatologists 9

cold 6–7, 8, 10–11, 15, 16, 18,20, 22

deserts 4, 9, 10, 14–15, 16, 20, 22

dry climates 4–5, 9, 10, 14–15, 16, 20

heat 4, 6–7, 8–9, 10, 12, 14–15, 16, 18, 20, 22

plants 10, 12–13, 14, 16

rain 4–5, 6, 8, 10, 12, 14–15, 16, 19, 20, 22

rain forests 10, 12–13, 22

snow 6–7, 8, 15, 16, 19

temperate 18–19

temperature 6, 8, 12, 14, 16, 18, 20

tropical climates 12, 22

tundra 16–17

water 14, 16, 22

weather 4, 6–7, 8, 18, 21

wet climates 10, 12, 20

Read More

Kalman, Bobbie, and Kelley MacAulay. *Changing Seasons.* New York: Crabtree Publishing (2005).

Murphy, Julie. *Desert Animal Adaptations.* Mankato, MN: Capstone (2012).

Learn More Online

To learn more about the climate, visit
www.bearportpublishing.com/WeatherWise

About the Author

Ellen Lawrence lives in the United Kingdom. Her favorite books to write are those about animals and nature. In fact, the first book Ellen bought for herself, when she was six years old, was the story of a gorilla named Patty Cake that was born in New York's Central Park Zoo.